How To  Items From Your Credit Report for FREE

How To Remove ALL Negative Items From Your Credit Report for FREE

A Do-It-Yourself Guide to Fixing your Credit Rating

by Riki Roash

DISCLAIMER

The author does not assume any responsibilities interpreting or implementing this book. This is not a legal advice.

It is based on her 18 years of most successful experience using this method to REMOVE ALL NEGATIVE DEROGATORY ITEMS from her and her client's credit report.

It is always a good idea to consult an attorney for a legal advice.

Table of Contents

Introduction

I have been in the financial planning business for over 18 years. I have also worked as a mortgage broker, simultaneously, on and off.

My clients would consult with me before buying a valuable asset, whether it's a new car or a house.

As part of my job and sense of loyalty to my clients and their families, I would help them correct their credit report, in order to receive a much better interest rate and save money. Although I happily did it free of charge, the satisfaction return was enormous. (Not to mention those clients stayed with me for years)

Now, correcting **inaccurate mistakes** reported on the credit report is a piece of cake. I am not talking about that.

I am talking about negative items that actually **do belong to you**, and prevent you from getting the house you desire, the new car or even a revolving credit card- line of credit that you need.

While credit repair companies and attorneys are charging an arm and a leg for it, you could do it yourself free of charge.

Well, maybe just the cost of this book (Which is less than a cup of coffee) and few dollars to make sure you have a proof you followed the process.

Yes, the secret of the credit repair companies is revealed. No more paying top dollar for this service. You can do it yourself for very close to nothing.

I want to make it clear. I do not own a credit repair business, nor do I refer you to one. This is not a referral business. This is merely secrets the professionals are using and charging lots of money for.

I decided to write this book to help you to have a good or even perfect credit score. After I looked at few books on the market, I realized they were written by people that either refer you to their website or a credit repair shop. It was just written to lure you to their business, in order to charge you for rapid re-score or credit repair service they provided. And this service comes with a hefty price tag.

I actually learned the details of correcting your credit legally and permanently, from an attorney that used to charge anywhere from $1500 to $3000 per client. Depends on the case, and the pocket of the client, I guess. If you think it's a lot of money now, it was for sure a lot of money years ago.

This attorney helped my client restore her credit from 528 to 689 Fico score. Just enough to get her approved for a loan I did for her, at a good rate, and save approximately $326 per month on mortgage (which represented a one and a half points charge, for the same interest rate she would of paid, if she didn't have 680 or better score). When I mentioned that $2600 is a lot of money, she replied: "If I don't correct my credit, I would pay approximately $118,000 over the life of the loan" which was 30 years.

Smart woman, she took my adviser role at that moment. (Although I have no doubt the attorney did the calculations for her).

Since I was the loan officer on her loan, I was part of the entire process. Not to mention that after she fixed her credit, she got a lower interest rate credit cards to pay off the current high bearing interest she had.

She returned a leased car and got a nicer newer leased car for cheaper, and saved on her homeowner insurance and car premium.

Easily few hundred dollars a month of savings. I also benefited from it, as she was a nurse and wanted to save for early retirement, so we invested most of her monthly savings in various investments.

Approximately ten years later, she had just over a hundred thousand dollars in her investments account. Not bad. Instead of spending this money on creditors due to bad credit...

She actually had the discipline to save it for her retirement.

When her daughter went to college she used some of this money to purchase a home where her daughter studied. Renting the four bedrooms to other girl-students from school. This paid for the mortgage, and even left approximately $250 every month for her daughter's spending cash.

Three years later, Her daughter finished school, and she sold the house for approximately $52,000 profit. She called me to reinvest it for her again.

Now, not every story is like this. However, **the difference in money savings between good or bad credit is huge.**

It adds up very quickly, to <u>a few thousand dollars</u> a year, easily!

This book **is not about rapid re-score**, that you need to prove the credit bureau made a mistake and you have the burden to provide all the exact certain requested documents to prove it, otherwise it is denied. Which also is a very expensive process.

Neither do you need cash to pay off credit cards to lower your debt ratio, which is used in rapid re-score very often. (It is actually an electronically filing with the bureaus to delete mistakes, or report the change in debt ratio rapidly. Which means you need the extra cash usually to achieve it. Instead of waiting a month or two from the creditor to show a payment, it calculates it quickly. Usually within five to seven business days.)

I will show you a way to **remove all negative items legally and permanently from your credit report.** The process we do today is more advanced and simple than it was years ago. You just need to know **exactly the right way to do it**, or the credit Bureau will deny your request.

If you have on your credit report:
collection accounts, charge offs, repos, bankruptcies, judgments, short-sales, loan modifications, late payments and any other negative derogatory items, then this program is for you. If you have a perfect credit-Stop reading now, it is not for you.

It is imperative to maintain a good credit Fico score for every day living necessities.
Are you **paying too much for car insurance?**
How about **homeowner or rental insurance?**
Have you been **denied a new credit card?**
Can't afford a **new car** due to bad credit?

Does your **dream house** stay only as a dream?

Does the **lender decline your mortgage loan** or charge you a much higher rate due to your credit score?

Will the **employer not hire you or give you a promotion** due to your bad credit?

Are you unable to **maintain your professional license** due to low Fico score?

Are you paying much more money every month for your mortgage, car, home and auto insurance premiums and credit cards?

You can save thousands of dollars a year if you fix your credit. You might invest this money and save it, or take a nice vacation and have extra money for you and your family.

It is easy.

I will show you a simple, legal way to force the credit bureaus to remove all negative items from your credit report permanently.

A step-by-step guide for a successful negative items removal. It works like a charm every time.

So what are you waiting for, shape the road to a better future-with a better credit for you and your family.

The Credit Bureaus

The main three bureaus in the United States are: Experian, Equifax and TransUnion.

Addresses for Credit Bureaus
Experian
P.O. Box 9556 Allen, TX 75013

Equifax
P.O. Box 740241 Atlanta, GA 30374-0241

TransUnion
P.O. Box 2000 Chester, PA 19022-2000

What's in your credit report?

Although each credit reporting agency formats and reports this information differently, all credit reports contain basically the same categories of information. Your social security number, date of birth and employment information are used to identify you. These factors are not used in credit scoring. Updates to this information come from information you supply to lenders.

Identifying Information.

Your name, address, Social Security number, date of birth and employment information are used to identify you. These factors are not used in credit scoring. Updates to this information come from information you supply to lenders.

Trade Lines.

These are your credit accounts. Lenders report on each account you have established with them. They report the type of account (bankcard, auto loan, mortgage, etc), the date you opened the account, your credit limit or loan amount, the account balance and your payment history.

Credit Inquiries.

When you apply for a loan, you authorize your lender to ask for a copy of your credit report. This is how inquiries appear on your credit report. The inquiries section contains a list of everyone who accessed your credit report within the last two years. The report you see lists both "voluntary" inquiries, spurred by your own requests for credit, and "involuntary" inquires, such as when lenders order your report so as to make you a pre-approved credit offer in the mail.

Public Record and Collection Items.

Credit reporting agencies also collect public record information from state and county courts, and information on overdue debt from collection agencies. Public record information includes bankruptcies, foreclosures, suits, wage attachments, liens and judgments.

What is a FICO score?

When you apply for credit – whether for a credit card, a car loan, or a mortgage – lenders want to know what risk they'd take by loaning money to you. **FICO scores are the credit scores most lenders use to determine your credit risk.**

You have three FICO scores, one for each of the three credit bureaus: **Experian, TransUnion, and Equifax.** Each score is based on information the credit bureau keeps on file about you. As this information changes, your credit scores tend to change as well. Your 3 FICO scores affect both how much and what loan terms (interest rate, etc.) lenders will offer you at any given time. Taking steps to improve your FICO scores can help you qualify for better rates from lenders.

For your three FICO scores to be calculated, each of your three credit reports must contain at least one account that has been open for at least six months. In addition, each report must contain at least one account that has been updated in the past six months. This ensures that there is enough information – and enough recent information – in your report on which to base a FICO score on each report. Credit bureau scores are often called **"FICO scores"** because most credit bureau scores used in the U.S. are **produced from software developed by Fair Isaac and Company**. FICO scores are provided to lenders by the major credit reporting agencies.

FICO scores are the best resource to determine the future credit risk. They are based solely on credit report data. **The higher the credit score, the lower the risk.** But no score says whether a specific individual will be a "good" or "bad" customer. And while many lenders use FICO scores to help them make lending decisions, each lender has its own strategy, including the level of risk it finds acceptable for a given credit product. There is no single "cutoff score" used by all lenders and there are many additional factors that lenders use to determine your actual interest rates. **Fico score ranges from 300 to 850 points.** A higher Fico score means less credit risk to the lender, which results in lower interest rates for you. Sometimes a few points can make a big difference. Coming from the mortgage and financial business, I saw it very often.

Many lenders require at least a 680 Fico score in order to receive a good rate mortgage or a car loan. Few points below and you are considered a higher credit risk consumer, which translates into a much higher interest rate.

There are many credit data that compose your Fico score. This data can be grouped into five categories as outlined below. The percentages in the chart reflect how important each of the categories is in determining your FICO score.

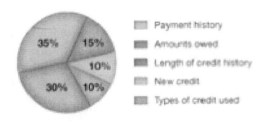

Payment History Account payment information on specific types of accounts (credit cards, retail accounts, installment loans, finance company accounts, mortgage, etc.)

Presence of adverse public records (bankruptcy, judgments, suits, liens, wage attachments, etc.), collection items, and/or delinquency (past due items)

Severity of delinquency (how long past due)

Amount past due on delinquent accounts or collection items

Time since (recency of) past due items (delinquency), adverse public records (if any), or collection items (if any)

Number of past due items on file

Number of accounts paid as agreed

Amounts Owed

Amount owing on accounts

Amount owing on specific types of accounts

Lack of a specific type of balance, in some cases

Number of accounts with balances

Proportion of credit lines used (proportion of balances to total credit limits on certain types of revolving accounts)

Proportion of installment loan amounts still owing (proportion of balance to original loan amount on certain types of installment loans)

Length of Credit History

Time since accounts opened

Time since accounts opened, by specific type of account

Time since account activity

New Credit

Number of recently opened accounts, and proportion of accounts that are recently opened, by type of account

Number of recent credit inquiries

Time since recent account opening(s), by type of account

Time since credit inquiry(s)

Re-establishment of positive credit history following past payment problems

Types of Credit Used

Number of (presence, prevalence, and recent information on) various types of accounts (credit cards, retail accounts, installment loans, mortgage, consumer finance accounts, etc.)

What is not considered in your Fico score:

Your race, color, religion, national origin, sex and marital status. US law prohibits credit scoring from considering these facts, as well as any receipt of public assistance, or the exercise of any consumer right under the Consumer Credit Protection Act.

Your age. Other types of scores may consider your age, but FICO scores don't.

Your salary, occupation, title, employer, date employed or employment history. Lenders may consider this information, however, as may other types of scores.

Where you live.

Any interest rate being charged on a particular credit card or other account.

Any items reported as child/family support obligations or rental agreements.

Certain types of inquiries (requests for your credit report). The score does not count "consumer-initiated" inquiries – requests you have made for your credit report, in order to check it. It also does not count "promotional inquiries" – requests made by lenders in order to make you a "pre-approved" credit offer – or "administrative inquiries" – requests made by lenders to review your account with them. Requests that are marked as coming from employers are not counted either.

Any information not found in your credit report.

Any information that is not proven to be predictive of future credit performance.

Whether or not you are participating in a credit counseling of any kind.

Credit Inquiries

Will my FICO score drop if I apply for new credit?

If it does, it probably won't drop much. If you apply for several credit cards within a short period of time, multiple inquiries will appear on your report. Looking for new credit can equate with higher risk, but most credit scores are not affected by multiple inquiries from auto, mortgage or student loan lenders within a short period of time. Typically, these are treated as a single inquiry and will have little impact on the credit score.

What is an "inquiry"?

When you apply for credit, you authorize those lenders to ask or "inquire" for a copy of your credit report from a credit bureau. When you later check your credit report, you may notice that their credit inquiries are listed. You may also see listed there inquiries by businesses that you don't know. But the only inquiries that count toward your FICO score are the ones that result from your applications for new credit.

Does applying for credit affect my FICO score?

Fair Isaac's research shows that opening several credit accounts in a short period of time represents greater credit risk. When the information on your credit report indicates that you have been applying for multiple new credit lines in a short period of time (as opposed to rate shopping for a single loan, which is handled differently as discussed below), your FICO score can be lower as a result.

How much will credit inquiries affect my score?

The impact from applying for credit will vary from person to person based on their unique credit histories. In general, credit inquiries have a small impact on one's FICO score. For most people, one additional credit inquiry will take less than five points off their FICO score. For perspective, the full range for FICO scores is 300-850. Inquiries can have a greater impact if you have few accounts or a short credit history. Large numbers of inquiries also mean greater risk. Statistically, people with six inquiries or more on their credit reports can be up to eight times more likely to declare bankruptcy than people with no inquiries on their reports. While inquiries often can play a part in assessing risk, they play a minor part. Much more important factors for your score are how timely you pay your bills and your overall debt burden as indicated on your credit report.

Does the formula treat all credit inquiries the same?

No. Research has indicated that the FICO score is more predictive when it treats loans that commonly involve rate-shopping, such as mortgage, auto and student loans, in a different way. For these types of loans, the FICO score ignores inquiries made in the 30 days prior to scoring. So, if you find a loan within 30 days, the inquiries won't affect your score while you're rate shopping.

In addition, the score looks on your credit report for rate-shopping inquiries older than 30 days. If it finds some, it counts those inquiries that fall in a typical shopping period as just one inquiry when determining your score.

For FICO scores calculated from older versions of the scoring formula, this shopping period is any 14-day span. For FICO scores calculated from the newest versions of the scoring formula, this shopping period is any 45day span. Each lender chooses which version of the FICO scoring formula it wants the credit reporting agency to use to calculate your FICO score.

What to know about "rate shopping."

Looking for a mortgage, auto or student loan may cause multiple lenders to request your credit report, even though you are only looking for one loan. To compensate for this, the score ignores mortgage, auto, and student loan inquiries made in the 30 days prior to scoring. So, if you find a loan within 30 days, the inquiries won't affect your score while you're rate shopping. In addition, the score looks on your credit report for mortgage, auto, and student loan inquiries older than 30 days. If it finds some, it counts those inquiries that fall in a typical shopping period as just one inquiry when determining your score. For FICO scores calculated from older versions of the scoring formula, this shopping period is any 14-day span. For FICO scores calculated from the newest versions of the scoring formula, this shopping period is any 45-day span. Each lender chooses which version of the FICO scoring formula it wants the credit reporting agency to use to calculate your FICO score.

Improving your FICO score.

If you need a loan, do your rate shopping within a focused period of time, such as 30 days. FICO scores distinguish between a search for a single loan and a search for many new credit lines, in part by the length of time over which inquiries occur.

Generally, people with high FICO scores consistently:
- Pay bills on time.
- Keep balances low on credit cards and other revolving credit products.

- Apply for and open new credit accounts only as needed.

Also, here are some good credit management practices that can help to raise your FICO score over time:

- Re-establish your credit history if you have had problems. Opening new accounts responsibly and paying them on time will raise your FICO score over the long term.
- Check your own credit reports regularly, before applying for new credit, to be sure they are accurate and up-to-date. As long as you order your credit reports through an organization authorized to provide credit reports to consumers, such as myFICO, your own inquiries will not affect your FICO score.

How to Order a Free Credit Report

Https://www.annualcreditreport.com **is the only official site to help consumers obtain their credit report free of charge.** This site is sponsored by the three major credit report bureaus, to furnish a free credit report annually as required by federal law.

If you didn't request a free credit report in the last 12 months, please do so through this website. It will contain a report of your credit from Experian, Equifax and TransUnion.

If you were denied credit, you have the right to request a free credit report within 60 days from the inquiry request. However it will be provided only by the certain credit bureau your credit report has used. For instance, if you applied for a credit card and received a letter of denial, the letter will specify which credit bureau the information was pulled from (Experian, Equifax or TransUnion). Information about the bureau is also included. You might want to write to them or call them.

You will need:
1. To make sure you are within the 60 days period, from date of inquiry.
2. The credit reporting agency that supplies the information. Mailing address and phone address, or website information must be listed on the letter.

3. To contact the bureau. You will need your social security number, name and address, and in many states a copy of your driver license. The date and creditor name that denied you credit.

Here are the three credit reporting bureaus in case you don't have it handy:

Equifax
- For a copy of your report:

P.O. Box 740241 Atlanta, GA 30374-0241   (800) 685-1111
- To dispute data in your report:

P.O. Box 740256 Atlanta, GA 30374-0256   (800) 216-1035 or (800) 685-5000
- To report credit fraud:

(800) 525-6285

<u>Experian</u>
- For a copy of your report:

P.O. Box 8030 Layton, UT 84041 (800) 682-7654
- To dispute data in your report:

P.O. Box 2106 Allen, TX 75013 (800) 422-4879
- To report credit fraud:

Fax- (800) 301-7195

<u>TransUnion</u>
- For a copy of your report:

P.O. Box 390 Springfield, PA 19064 (800) 916-8800
- To dispute data in your report:

P.O. Box 34012 Fullerton, CA 92634 (800) 916-8800
- To report credit fraud:

(800) 916-8800

Once you ordered your credit report **analyze it carefully.**

Many times there are mistakes in the credit report.

How credit report mistakes are made

When a credit report contains errors, it is often because the report is incomplete, or contains information about someone else. This typically happens because:

- The person applied for credit under different names (Robert Jones, Bob Jones, etc.).
- Someone made a clerical error in reading or entering name or address information from a hand-written application.
- The person gave an inaccurate Social Security number, or the number was misread by the lender.
- Loan or credit card payments were inadvertently applied to the wrong account.

HOW TO REMOVE MISTAKES FROM YOUR CREDIT REPORT

The Fair Credit Reporting Act (FCRA) is designed to help ensure that credit bureaus furnish correct and complete information to businesses to use when evaluating your application. Hence,

Those mistakes are easy to remove, as the Fair credit act requires the bureaus to remove all inaccurate information on one's credit report.

You will need:
1. A copy of your credit report.
2. You need your social security number
3. Clearly identify each item in your report you dispute.
4. State the facts and explain why you dispute the information.
5. Request a deletion from your report, as the law requires.

Your letter may look like this:

Your Name
Your Address
Your City, State, Zip Code
Date
Complaint Department
Name of Credit Bureau
Address
City, State, Zip Code

RE: Inaccurate information on my credit report.
Dear Sirs:
I am writing to dispute the following information on my credit report. The items I dispute also are encircled on the attached copy of the report I received.
The following items are incorrect:
1. Account number, Credit account
2. Judgment or creditor or tax court.
Those items are inaccurate. They do not belong to me.
I am requesting that the items be deleted. By the FCRA you have thirty days to conduct an investigation. Any information which is not 100% accurate, must be deleted.

Sincerely,
Your name
Enclosures: (List what you are enclosing,
like a copy of your credit report)

The credit bureau must investigate the items within thirty days, and delete it from your report unless they were able to verify the items. Or, unless they found your request frivolous. A letter of the outcome from their investigation should be sent to you.

Also, a **new credit report** with the changes must be provided for you free of charge, and not count as an inquiry against you.

<u>**Send a certified letter, return receipt requested,**</u> and keep a copy of the letter and the post office receipt for your

records. This will prove the credit bureau received your correspondence.

How to remove ALL negative Items from your report

The credit bureaus are private "For profit" companies (as opposed to "non-profit" organizations). It is approximately a four billion dollar business. The bureaus have a legal responsibility to comply with the Fair Credit Reporting Act, and follow the law that protects the consumers.

The credit bureaus are allowed to have negative items on the credit report only if it is 100% accurate and also verifiable.

Accurate means that all the information is correct: The date the account was opened. The amount owed is exact and correct. Account number matches your account number, and so on.

It has been reported that the credit bureaus have over 70% mistakes on the credit report files. Chances are that your report has inaccurate information and you can dispute it.

The credit bureau also must make sure the information reported is verifiable to the consumer, upon request. **Within 15 days after investigation results completed.**

The credit bureaus are required to provide the method of verification that includes the name, address, and telephone number of the data furnisher if requested by a consumer. Also, they must prove they received from the creditor a copy of original dated contract with your signature on it.

The good news is that the Bureaus are mostly not complying with the Fair Credit Reporting Act. They use automated system.

The standard dispute process has been automated by the credit bureaus through various electronic methods, the most common being **e-Oscar**, which is a centralized dispute communication tool. The dispute is usually scanned and processed out of the country, where labor is cheaper. Then it is assigned a two-digit e-Oscar code.

You, as the consumer, have the right to request a **method of verification proof.**

When you utilize the "Method of Verification" letter request, it can prove to be a very useful tool in your credit repair process.

This request is designed to force the credit reporting agencies to comply with the law during their investigation. Seeing as how most investigations are automated, requesting a MOV (Method of Verification) will often alert the credit reporting agencies that they have a smart consumer to deal with.

The credit Bureaus mostly do not follow the law, therefore, they usually do not have the verifiable information. To this date, as many requests as I have made with the credit bureaus, I had never received for me or my clients the verifiable requested information.

Bad news is that the credit Bureaus usually do not comply with the Fair Credit Reporting Act Law.

Good news is you can force them to do so. Hence, **remove any unverifiable negative information from your credit report permanently.**

This method of credit repair does not just claim "This negative item is not mine", or "This negative item is inaccurate".

It is much more powerful! It claims:
"**You, the credit bureaus, do not follow the law, therefore, you must delete the item** which is unverifiable or I will file a complaint with the Federal Trade Commission, the agency that regulates the credit bureaus".

I had a situation that I tried to remove a judgment for a client. It took me two dispute letters and a "Promise" this will go to the FTC before it worked. So don't give up. The credit bureau needs to delete the item if it cannot be satisfactorily verified.

This Method of Verification request is done only after you sent a letter of dispute and received a "Verified" or "New information below" response from the credit bureaus.

Never use the electronic internet dispute on the credit bureaus website.

You relinquish many important, necessary rights. By agreeing to the terms and conditions, you agree that if a disputed item returned "verified", you have no right to re-dispute this item again.

You also need the certified letter, with delivery confirmation, if you will need to file a complaint with the FTC. Usually, the credit bureaus will rather delete the items than waste time corresponding with the FTC.

The steps to remove ALL your negative items

Please follow these steps carefully:

Step 1:

Write a letter of dispute, and send it to each bureau. (Address was provided in previous chapter).

It is important you send a letter to each of the main credit bureaus; **Equifax, Experian and TransUnion**. It will be devastating to delete an item in one bureau, just to have it surface on the other one.

I would like you to know that the credit bureaus use a computer system to scan your letter.

If it is an internet template, they can stop the investigation before it arrived to its destination, and send you a denial letter with a frivolous reason or so.
DO NOT USE INTERNET TEMPLATES.
It is better if you hand write your dispute in a blue or black pen, or change the following sample a little bit to your own wording.

Here is a sample of a dispute letter:

Sample dispute letter to send to credit bureaus: (Round 1)

Name

Address
City, State, Zip Code
DOB & SSN
[Insert Credit Bureau]
Address
City, State, Zip Code
Date
RE: Inaccurate information on my credit report. S.S#000-00-0000

I am writing this letter to dispute the following listed accounts:

1. *Chase, Account #4343434*
2. *Capital bank, Charge off account #45343*

Due to the inaccuracy of this information, I request you to delete it from my file.

Be advised that the description of the procedure used to determine the accuracy and completeness of the information is hereby requested as well, to be provided within 15 days of the completion of your reinvestigation. Under federal law, you have 30 days to complete your reinvestigation.

Thank you in advance for your immediate attention to this matter.

Sincerely,
Your Name

It usually takes about 30 days to receive a response, although I have seen responds in about 20 days previously, and as long as 40 days.

If the credit Bureau responded with "Deleted" letter. Great! Congratulations. Mission accomplished. That was exactly our goal.

However, If one Bureau deleted and the others did not, **write only on step 2 to the ones who sent you a verified or other explanation letter.**

<u>Do not write back to the bureau regarding the deleted negative items</u>.

We don't want to reopen an investigation. You are done with them. Unless the credit bureau had some accounts deleted and some not, which I have experienced before. Write on round 2 **<u>only</u>** on the undeleted items.

I had a client with 16 negative items. One Bureau sent 13 "deleted", and two items "Verified", and one item they just neglected all together.

In round two, the Method of Verification letter, we tackled only the two verified items and the one that was completely neglected. We will not mention the deleted ones, as we achieved our goal satisfactorily.

<u>Step 2:</u>

<u>Method of Verification letter:</u>

Name
Address
City/State/Zip Code
Date
RE: Request to provide Method of Verification
To Whom It May Concern:

On [Insert Original Dispute Date] I requested an investigation because I felt the item is not being reported legally, and on [Insert Date of Response] I received a letter stating that your investigation was complete. Please answer the following questions:

What certified documents were reviewed to conclude your investigation?

Please provide me a complete copy of all of the information that was transmitted to the data furnisher as part of the investigation, as required by FCRA: · Who did you speak with? · What was the date? · How long was the conversation? · What was their position? · What number did you call? · What is the name of your employee that spoke directly to the creditor? · What is the position of your employee that spoke to the creditor?

This inaccurate reporting has caused me severe financial and emotional distress.

Please reply within 15 days to the above questions, or delete the items.

Sincerely,
Your name
DOB
S.S. # and address

Step3:

Sample Letter of a complaint with the FTC:

If you don't get the desired response after this letter, send a third letter:

Letter of intent to complain to the FTC if the issue is not resolved.

(Name and Address Here)
(Credit Bureau Department and Address Here)

(Date)

RE: Follow-up Dispute Letter of (insert date of original validation request letter)

NOTICE OF INTENT TO FILE COMPLAINT
To Whom It May Concern:
This letter shall serve as formal notice of my intent to file a complaint with the FTC, due to your disregard of the law.

You claim to have somehow verified the items I requested. Therefore, I legally requested a description of the procedures used to verify the information.

As indicated by the attached copy of the letter and mailing receipt [Insert Date on Receipt], you received and accepted through registered mail my request letter dated [Insert Date of Your Letter]. To date you have not responded to this request and have thus not performed your duty mentioned in the law.

Federal law requires you to respond within 15 days, yet you have failed to respond and it has been over 30 days. Failure to comply with these federal regulations by credit reporting agencies is investigated by the Federal Trade Commission (see 15 USC 41, et seq.).

I am maintaining a careful record of my communications with you on this matter; for the purpose of filing a complaint with the FTC, unless I hear from you in 20 days.

For the record, the following information is being erroneously included on my credit report.

[List all company name(s) and account number(s)]

You claimed to have verified the erroneous information, yet you refuse to tell me HOW you were able to verify these accounts. If you do not immediately remove this inaccurate and/or incomplete information, I will file a formal complaint with the FTC. As I stated, I am carefully documenting these events, including the lack of response REQUIRED under federal law from you. Any further delay is inexcusable.

Sincerely,
Your Name
S.S.#

I never had to go further. Usually just the "intent to file a complaint with the FTC" works. However, if this doesn't work, you might want to file a real complaint with FTC, and let them investigate.

Remember:

Patience is of the essence. However it is worth it. To see the credit card invitations with zero interest rate arriving in the mail.

Refinance offers and car dealer offers arriving in the mail is a real pleasure. You know your credit is fixed, and you are credit worthy, and categorized as a low credit risk consumer.

Instead of the method of verification letter, I have tried in the past to write a second time to the credit bureau with a dispute letter, advising them that the information by FCRA must be 100% accurate, and it is not. They need to respond within 30 days. Since they are receiving approximately ten thousand letters in a day, they don't respond to all of them, and therefore delete the items. You might want to try that too.

Some attorneys send the letter of dispute a few times, waiting three to seven days in between. It is working, but the method of verification letter is more powerful, and has worked better in my past experiences.

What to do with Harassing collection agencies

People are convinced to make a small payment to a creditor that is harassing them, to keep them "off their back" so to speak. When the creditor or collection agency realizes the statue of limitation is approaching in your state, (different states have different periods), they are desperate to receive **any** kind of monetary value from you, in order to keep the **debt "alive"**.

This means that if you have a credit card debt and your state has a four year statue of limitation, when the four year mark approaches, if you pay even one dollar to the creditor, you start a new four year of statue of limitation.

It is either from the last bill paid, or the new payment of one dollar you made. This gives power to the creditor to sue you, for another four years. If you didn't pay anything for the four years, and the creditor sues you, you can come to court and throw it out by proving the statue of limitation had passed, or send a certified letter to the attorney suing you requesting to cease the suit right away as it passed the statue of limitation in your state.

A debt that passed the statue of limitation is also known as a "**Zombie debt**".

Another way to stop the collection agencies harassing you, is **requesting a debt validation proof from the collection agency**. By law they need to provide it to you within 30 days.

Another way to remove negative items legally

LETTER OF DEBT VALIDATION

Under the **Federal Debt Collection Practices Act,** you are allowed to **challenge the validity of a debt that a collection agency states you owe them.**

People neglect to request a debt validation proof from the collection agency. Collection agencies usually do not keep a written copy of your debt contract. They usually buy the debts in bulk for pennies on the dollar.

If you are getting sued, or being harassed by the collection agency, you write them a **letter requesting a debt validation proof**.

I used it on one client when he brought the summons to me all frightened. The lawsuit stopped and the phone calls stopped. It doesn't mean you don't owe the debt. It means there is a quiet period until this info is provided to you. Until this date he never received one.

Do not settle for a computer print. You want to see a written **contract with your signature on it. Date, amount and all of detailed information**. You have the right to receive it.

If the creditor does not provide it for you, they can not sue you, or contact you until it's provided.

This is a sample letter to the collection agency.

Make the agency verify that the debt is actually yours and owed by you.

Keep a copy for your files and send the letter registered mail, with a delivery receipt.

Date
Your Name
Your Address
City, State Zip
Collection Agency
Collection Agency Address
City, State Zip

Re: Acct # XXXX-XXXX-XXXX-XXXX

To Whom It May Concern:
I am sending this letter to you in response to a notice I received from you on (date of letter). Be advised, this is not a refusal to pay, but a notice sent pursuant to the Fair Debt Collection Practices Act, 15 USC 1692g Sec. 809 (b) that your claim is disputed and validation is requested.

This is NOT a request for "verification" or proof of my mailing address, but a request for VALIDATION made pursuant to the above named Title and Section. I respectfully request that your office provide me with competent evidence that I have any legal obligation to pay you.

Please provide me with the following:
- *What the money you say I owe is for;*
- *Explain and show me how you calculated what you say I owe;*
- *Provide me with copies of any papers that show I agreed to pay what you say I owe;*
- *Provide a verification or copy of any judgment if applicable;*

- *Identify the original creditor;*
- *Prove the Statute of Limitations has not expired on this account;*
- *Show me that you are licensed to collect in my state; and*
- *Provide me with your license numbers and Registered Agent.*

If your offices have reported invalidated information to any of the three major Credit Bureau's (Equifax, Experian or TransUnion), said action might constitute fraud under both Federal and State Laws. Due to this fact, if any negative mark is found on any of my credit reports by your company or the company that you represent I will not hesitate in bringing legal action against you for the following:

- *Violation of the Fair Credit Reporting Act*
- *Violation of the Fair Debt Collection Practices Act*
- *Defamation of Character*

If your offices are able to provide the proper documentation as requested, I will require at least 30 days to investigate this information and during such time all collection activity must cease and desist.

Also during this validation period, if any action is taken which could be considered detrimental to any of my credit reports, I will consult with my legal counsel. This includes any information to a credit reporting repository that could be inaccurate or invalidated or verifying an account as accurate when in fact there is no provided proof that it is.

If your offices fail to respond to this validation request within 30 days from the date of your receipt, all references to this account must be deleted and completely removed from my credit file and a copy of such deletion request shall be sent to me immediately.

I would also like to request, in writing, that no telephone contact be made by your offices to my home or to my place of employment. If your offices attempt telephone communication with me, including but not limited to computer generated calls or correspondence sent to any third parties, it will be considered harassment and I will have no choice but to file suit. All future communications with me MUST be done in writing and sent to the address noted in this letter.

This is an attempt to correct your records, any information obtained shall be used for that purpose.

Sincerely

Your Signature

Your Name

Step2:

Once you have requested the debt validation letter from the collection agency, and have not receive it, you **write back to the collection agency requesting the removal of the item from the credit report,** as they are in violation of the FDCPA, section 809 (b).

Step 3:

If the collection agency **removes the item -Great!**

If the collection agency does not reply to your removal request,
You contact the credit bureau.
You write to the credit bureau a letter requesting to remove the item from the credit report, with a copy of

the letter you sent to the creditor, requesting to remove the item since no validation proof was given.

I prefer to work directly with the credit bureau, rather than dealing with the creditor or collection agency. In the past, it worked for me the best. If you are persistent, the credit bureau will be forced to remove those negative items permanently. It might require another letter, but usually when they receive the FTC complaint letter warning , they delete the items.

Don't forget the credit bureau receives about 10000 letters a day. They are for profit organizations. They want to be as quick and cost effective as possible. That's why they send the complaint to cheaper labor countries, and mostly use the e-Oscar electronic system.

When the credit bureau sees a smart consumer, they would rather delete the item than risk receiving complaints with the FTC. At least, that was my experience in the past years.

Nevertheless, since the credit bureaus do not follow the FCRA rules and fail to provide a solid legitimate detailed verifiable proof to the consumer most of the time, you are able to delete all of the negative items on your credit report legally and permanently. You can also sue them for a $1000 penalty, since they are in violation of the FDCPA, section 809 (b), and FCRA 611(a) rule.

Bonus: 10 Mistakes to avoid while repairing your credit

1. Do not give any **additional detailed** information to the credit bureaus about the **negative item**. For instance: Do not write: The collection agency is showing $1200, but I owe only $200. The credit bureau would change the sum, but the negative item will stay. Remember, the bureau must have 100% accurate information. If the item shows $1200 rather than $200 it is inaccurate. It is enough to say "this item is inaccurate".

2. Always **certify mail, with delivery return receipt all your correspondence with the credit bureau**. In case you need to file a claim or a lawsuit, you need the paper trail and proof you sent the claim.

3. Always keep a **copy of all correspondence for your records.**

4. **Never utilize the electronic dispute request on the credit bureau websites.** You give up your rights. By agreeing to the terms on their website you relinquish your rights. If an item is denied or verified, **you can not re-dispute it again**. Also, the credit bureau does not have to respond to you back in writing. Case closed. It seems to be more comfortable, but it is very costly. Stick to the old fashioned way of correspondence. That is letters.

5. **Do not close credit cards that you don't need. Your debt ratio will go up, and might reduce your credit score.** Keep all accounts open. Use it for a

small amount once a month, and pay for it in full when you get the statement.

6. **Try to pay your credit cards in full every month if possible.** That will show you are a low risk credit consumer, and able to manage your finances well.

7. **Ask the credit card company to extend your line of credit limit**. If they need to check your credit-skip it. It might affect your score.

8. **Do not use internet templates for your dispute**. It can be denied as frivolous by the credit Bureau, before it reached its destination. Use it as a sample and change the wording, or use the samples here, and also change it a little bit.

9. **Check your credit for free at least once a year,** and stay on top of your credit report. You might discover new items just in time to fix it.

10. **People fail to reestablish their credit**. If you were refused a credit card. Find a bank or a credit company that will allow you to deposit money in an account, and extend a line of credit for the same amount. Request them to report it to the credit bureaus, so you will show an open revolving line of credit.

And most importantly:
Do not give up easily! People stop the process too soon.

Sometimes all you need is one extra letter. It never took me more than three letters. Usually the first or second will do. Especially if a complaint to the FTC or hiring an attorney is mentioned.

So be patient!

I wish you good luck to a new and better future credit. You and your family deserve it!

The author and editor have invested much time in making this book available to you. I hope you have gained important knowledge from this book, and have learned how you can remove all negative items from your credit report permanently and legally. A positive review would be much appreciated. Thank you in advance. ;-)

This book and the ebook version are available on
www.amazon.com

Made in the USA
San Bernardino, CA
14 April 2015